The Perfect
Human Capital Storm

The Perfect Human Capital Storm

Workplace Human Capital Challenges and Opportunities in the 21st Century

Implications for Organizations and Leaders,
2nd edition

Edwin Mouriño-Ruiz

INFORMATION AGE PUBLISHING, INC.
Charlotte, NC • www.infoagepub.com

Library of Congress Cataloging-in-Publication Data

A CIP record for this book is available from the Library of Congress
http://www.loc.gov

ISBN: 978-1-68123-867-8 (Paperback)
         978-1-68123-868-5 (Hardcover)
         978-1-68123-869-2 (ebook)

Dedication

I want to first dedicate this book to the Almighty, because through Him everything is possible and without Him nothing is. I want to thank Him for allowing me this journey on this earth and for the experiences He has given me. Thanks also to my grandparents and mother (the Ruiz family), who made me the man I am today; to my bride, wife, and love of my life, who has served as my rock as I journey through the good and bad of the corporate experience; to those whom I've worked with who have served as true friends in my working experience; and finally, to those whom I supported, consulted, educated, and coached in order to help them help themselves in their corporate journey and work life.

Contents

Foreword

Edwin has developed a marvelous primer on eight critical forces that are facing organizations these days. These forces, if managed properly, can make a huge difference in the organization. If these forces are not managed properly, they can result in disaster. We are all witnessing the effects of these forces. In some cases, they are consuming us and inhibiting performance, but it does not have to be that way.

The first three forces focus on the demographics and what we must do as organizations and as a society to address this. An aging workforce means that people will now be working longer, and they will need healthcare and retirement benefits for more years. This could be a burden on organizations and society. Demographics are changing in terms of ethnic groups throughout this country. The individuals who comprise our workforce are changing rapidly, and if this change is not integrated properly into the system, it can be disastrous. The concept of diversity has changed. Previously, we thought of diversity as making sure we had the right people in the right jobs to be in compliance and improve our image. This prevented people from being upset because they were not included, and prevented them from leaving, making complaints, or filing charges. This is the old way of thinking. The new way of thinking is to consider a diverse workforce as a much better workforce, a workforce that can be more productive, more innovative, and produce higher quality products and services. Having four generations in the workplace is both interesting and challenging. The new way of thinking

The Perfect Human Capital Storm, pages ix–xii

is to see this as an opportunity to make a difference, to make contributions, and to be more productive.

Each one of the forces that Edwin describes has a positive side and a dark side. For technology, the bright side is that it makes us more productive, it speeds up all types of processes, improves communications, lowers costs, and can actually eliminate the need for hiring additional people. The dark side is that it may eliminate jobs at a time when we need more jobs. Technology can also be misused and abused in organizations, inhibiting productivity instead of enhancing it. Technology makes companies subject to cyber-attacks. Consider the effect of the cyber-attack on Target stores. Those attacks tarnished the image of Target, led to rapid declines in its stock price, affected overall sales, and reduced the retirement nest egg for many Target employees. Technology must be addressed properly and fairly.

Edwin describes these forces as important challenges, if we do nothing. These challenges can affect the business in a negative way. But if they are addressed with positive solutions, they can make a huge difference. Each challenge is an opportunity to be explored and addressed. Edwin finishes each chapter with implications for organizations.

Most of the data presented in this book are lists of facts and trends that are often astonishing, provocative, and truly amazing. Yet, the key is to actually do something about these forces. While the actions must be driven by top organizational leaders and sometimes by political and community groups, the bulk of action rests with the human resources function. The human resources officer in an organization is charged with addressing these challenges, but too often this is not working. When you examine most organizations, the human capital strategy focuses on the day-to-day issues of attracting the best employees, paying them fairly, motivating them for higher performance, and keeping them with the organization for a long period of time. That is the old way of thinking. The new way of thinking is to address these issues, while at the same time having proactive approaches with the changes in demographics, technology, employee engagement, and other forces. We have to make up the short falls of education or work with the educational system to make it effective. We must grow outstanding global leaders in organizations who can make a difference. All of this focuses on bringing change. The new human capital strategy must define what the organization will do in each of these areas in terms of policy, strategy, and proposed actions.

Individuals in HR have had many wake-up calls, and this is yet another one. While Edwin addresses eight forces, there are even more forces that can be minefields if not addressed properly. These include employee health and wellness, the effects of globalization, and the effects of energy and the environment. The point is there are many forces that can make a difference, and the HR's function and the HR leader must guide the organization into appropriate strategies and actions to make it work.

We think you will enjoy this primer on these eight forces. More importantly, this book will stimulate you to take action to do something about them.

—Jack Phillips

What's Different in This 2nd Edition?

The differences in this 2nd edition are the order of the trends and topics. This order makes the storyline and the case for change flow easier, makes more logical sense, and builds a better case for the reasons why these trends are not only individually but collectively important. This edition adds new content and insights to each of the trends, particularly in the technology and education sections. This edition also provides a more comprehensive set of recommendations in order to address these challenges and opportunities for organizations. Lastly, this edition includes a survey for organizations to take in order to assess their respective organization when it comes to how effectively they are addressing these trends and changes causing their organizations to evolve.

Let's begin.

1

The Setting

The workplace as we know it is changing around us. As the environment changes, there is arguably no time more important for leaders, managers, and supervisors at all levels to truly demonstrate effective leadership behaviors. The 21st century has brought some interesting challenges and opportunities for organizations and their workforces. We are no longer in the manufacturing era of the 20th century.

While in the 20th century there were plenty of organizational changes taking place through mergers, acquisitions, downsizing, and outsourcing, most leaders would probably agree that these changes were not to the extent of the organizational change that has occurred since 2000 through now. There are several reasons for this acceleration of change, including the exponential growth of technology along with a globally, growing, connected environment and an aging population. This ever-changing business climate has positioned organizations to either capitalize on these changes, or be left behind and cease to exist in the future. At the core (and most importantly), leadership has and will continue to play a key role in these changes.

The Perfect Human Capital Storm, pages 1–4

Leadership has been studied for many years in different contexts and settings. This book is written from the perspective of a student, observer, educator, and adviser/consultant of leaders in workplace dynamics. It was written from the perspective of one who has worked for various organizations and in several industries for nearly 40 years.

The organizations I have worked for have made various attempts to strengthen leadership and employee development, and continue to do so, while trying to create a positive culture. Executives have tried to position their companies to achieve business objectives and improve the bottom line, while working to adapt to the changing environment around them. Some were successful, while many others appeared to just be going through the motions. Those that have been ineffective have been so by having ineffective leadership that is providing limited if any support to issues like diversity, ineffective change efforts, and downsizing while professing to be working to create an engaged workforce. Today's workplace psychology is transitioning toward one where workers are craving meaning and purpose in life, yet few are finding this at work. In essence, the workforce's expectations are changing, yet many organizations are not adapting fast enough to meet these changing expectations (MacKay & Sisodia, 2014).

The following is written from a high-level, almost tip-of-the-iceberg perspective. Each of the areas addressed could be its own book topic. However, these changes are happening at the same time, and the combination of changes creates interesting implications, challenges, and opportunities for organizations. All of these changes occurring simultaneously can be overwhelming.

So while I will not do justice from a depth perspective on each topic or trend, that is not the intent of this book. Instead, the intent is to show how the topics when looked at from a combined perspective: provide opportunities for the leadership of organizations to pause and create not only an organizational strategy as executives to reinvent their companies in their particular industries and markets, but also to create a human capital strategy for their organizations and their future.

The Perfect Storm

Education is what people do to you; learning is what you do to yourself.
—Joi Ito (TED Talk, 2014)

This quote highlights the dual intent of this book. My intent is to provide insight and to educate the reader on what is occurring; along with, and more importantly, my belief and hope that each reader will take away their own respective learning, depending on where they are in their career, their respective organization, and industry. There is a perfect storm brewing globally and nationally, particularly in regards to workplace implications, during the next decade and beyond. It consists of several variables, increasing in pace and importance over time. These factors might seem overwhelming to address all at the same time, but they are factors that organizations need to face because they are not going away. How leaders focus on them will mean the difference between the success of an organization and the evolution of an industry or enterprise.

According to Casio, "The following trends suggest that old approaches to managing the workforce may no longer be appropriate responses to economic or social reality" (Casio, 2015). These trends have implications for organizations and in turn for leaders at all levels. As society continues to age, demographics also continue to change. What is enabling these trends is that we are working and living in a volatile, uncertain, complex, and ambigious (VUCA) globally competitive environment. VUCA emerged as a concept from the military in the 1990s (Slocum, 2013) as the military tried to work in and through their uncertain and constantly changing and unexpected environments.

These changes mean that terms like *minority* and *majority* will evolve in the 21st century, particularly in the United States. The United States presently has four age groups in the workforce. Education will increasingly become more important as higher education will be required for the higher-level skills in the workplace. Technology continues and will continue to grow and change at exponential levels. Employee engagement continues to gain importance, especially during these changing and tough economic times. Leadership and leadership development will increasingly become fundamental for the success of organizations. All of the previously mentioned will force organizational change to remain constant, since organizations will need to adapt to the ever-changing environment in order to stay ahead of their competitors.

All of these trends and changes are happening at the same time, while organizations work to stay ahead of their competitors. Globalization and technology are two factors that are forcing organizations to step back and rethink how they will move forward in these fast-paced times. If society has learned anything by now, especially in the early stages of the 21st century, it is that we can no longer say that something will not happen.

Since 2000, there have been many technological and overall societal changes that we probably had not considered, even in the late 20th century.

Few people, if anyone, back in 2000 ever thought a tragedy like 9/11 could occur; or from a more practical and business perspective that a shifting paradigm would bring the start-up of Uber, Airbnb, Netflix, or Amazon. These new business models would change how organizations do business in what would become part of past traditional business practices. The enterprise of the 21st century will have to operate differently in order to succeed (Roehrig & Pring, 2012).

These few previous examples have led to ensuring that organizations are developing their organizational strategy, their companies, and their leadership teams at all levels in order to create a human capital strategy that enables a culture that will support these changes and position companies for success. Organizations that take their eyes off of any one of these areas do so at their own risk. The challenge and opportunity is how organizations address and work through this perfect storm.

Let us begin by looking at these trends and the implications for organizations, then the United States and finally the world.

2

Organizational Change

You must be the change you wish to see in the world.
—Mahatma Gandhi (Wildmind.org, 2006)

Organizations find themselves continually having to adapt, evolve, and reinvent themselves in order to position themselves competitively. This is primarily due to how organizational change is increasing and speeding up—enabled by emerging markets, mergers and acquisitions—and the driving need to have an innovative and creative workplace in order to thrive, and for organizations to reinvent themselves.

Recently, it was identified that there are 16 trends impacting the global environment. These range from an aging global population, decreasing tech learners, employees spending less time at work, to countries looking to attract and retain talent, and the growing trend requiring work flexibility (Indeed, 2016). In addition, there is the changing mindset of the organizational employee where more so now then ever before, the typical employee craves meaning and purpose in life, but few are finding this fullfillment at work (Mackey & Sisodia, 2014).

The Perfect Human Capital Storm, pages 5–8
Copyright © 2017 by Information Age Publishing

5

For organizations not recognizing—and unfortunately too many have not—this change of not keeping pace with this expected employee attitude about work will place these organizations at a disadvantage. This is not helped by research indicating that employees are usually productive little more than 60% of their workday; while during organizational change, productivity can potentially drop down to 15% (Pritchett & Pounds, 2008).

How well organizations manage change is not always seen as a positive due to the continual problems organizations have in dealing with change. Technological insertions, strategy implementation, failed IT project management, downsizing, outsourcing, along with difficulties in mergers have sometimes created more losses then gains for shareholders.

Organizations will need to continue to learn how to adapt and change or face an "extinction event," as cited in the book *Code Halos* (Frank, Roehrig, & Pring, 2014). An extinction event is described as the phenomena of a company going out of business because they have ignored the significance of transition their competitors have made, usually technologically.

To highlight this point, keep in mind that today only 70 of the Fortune 500 that appeared in 1955 still exist, and nearly 2,000 companies have come and gone since then. While these changes have occurred, the corporate life expectancy of the Fortune 500 has gone from 61 years in 1958 to 20 years today (Murray, 2015). This is further reinforced today by companies like Borders, Circuit City (once highlighted in the book *Good to Great* as an excellent company), Woolworth, and others that have come and gone due to a blatant disregard for changing their ways to keep up with the changing business models. Since 2000, we have organizations with new business models and organizational cultures like Twitter, Whatsapp, Uber, Amazon, Pandora, LinkedIn, and others that have welcomed the change instead of neglecting it after starting up.

Add to this, things like technology that is automating many portions of work where there is a growing contingent workforce, and organizational structures that are being forced to change (Bersin, 2016b). This is creating an uncertain future for organizations and work in general.

In the 21st century, organizations will not need a lot of physical capital, but smarter technological infrastrucuture. This can be seen already today: Uber provides a car service without owning any automobiles, and AirBnB provides rooms without owning any real estate and hotels. The increasingly important capital will be the human capital (Murray, 2015). All of these changes are up against the backdrop of change management effectiveness that has remained steady at only 30% from 1995 to 2010 (Cummings &

Worley, 2008). Much has been written about the need to change behaviors in order to instill a winning culture. But what will it really take?

Leaders need to remember that for organizations to change, there needs to be effective leadership committed to guiding and supporting the change with a clear and shared vision of the future. In addition, they need to ensure they are equipping the workforce with the appropriate skills needed in the changing organization along with a clear incentive for implementing the change. People want to know "What's in it for me," the famous FM station that we all tune into when asked to commit to something (otherwise known as WIIFM). Finally, employees will need the resources in order to be successful with a clear action plan as to how they will achieve the organizational changes.

Over the years, people have provided some form of resistance to change. Superiors may think these workers are inept, but the reality is that their resistance to change might be for good reasons. Usually this resistance to change is due to one of three (if not all three) reasons. The three reasons for resistance are because they don't understand it, like it, or like the individual creating the change. It could be that he or she does not *understand* the change. Here, it is the role of the leader to ensure that the individual understands the rationale for why the change must be done. It could also be that the individual might not *like* the change. He or she does not see the value of the change or agree with it. Finally, it could be that the person may not like *who* is driving the change. This comes down to trusting the individual trying to implement the change (Maurer, 2010).

When a manager establishes a culture of "my way or the highway," it minimizes genuine buy-in to the change. In turn, the organization gains passive-aggressive behavior or just resistance to the change (Merchant, 2011). There has been much written about the culture needed in order to implement an organizational change or strategic effort, so much so that there are articles highlighting the idea that culture trumps strategy every time. Another way I've read this described is that "culture eats strategy for lunch."

A recent interview with the CEO of Starbucks, Howard Schultz, highlighted aspects of this. When asked to what he attributed his organization's success, he stated, "The secret sauce to our success is the culture and values of our company" (Bartiromo, 2013). This was previously mentioned by former Southwest CEO Herb Kelleher who stated, "Everything [in our strategy] our competitors could copy tomorrow. But they can't copy the culture—they know it." In another organization, Veritas, the organization's founding CEO, Mark Leslie, credited his company's beginning success to a culture of transparency (DuBrin, 2014).

This just reinforces the point that organizational changes make leadership development that much more of an imperative, so that leaders are equipped to guide their organizations and workforce through what could be potentially difficult times. While this might provide a challenge, it also provides an opportunity.

So What Can an Organization Do?

The following are some considerations and recommendations.

Organizations need to create an environment of transparency and in turn make the case for change. Organizations need to educate their leaders and workforce on how to adapt to change, ensure everyone understands the reason for the change, and ensure the workforce is part of the change. Organizations will need to ensure they are attracting the right talent and creating an organizational culture of retaining and developing them (Royal & Stark, 2016).

In addition, there needs to be a supportive culture of accountability and rewards for supporting the organization through change. This is something that needs to be part of the human capital investment for the long run of the organization. Transparency and education will be key to helping the workforce understand why changes need to occur, and will grasp the importance of ongoing changes due to changing technology, external competition, and shifting work arrangements and expectations.

Lastly, organizations should consider following Kotter's eight steps to effective change (Kotter, 2007). This includes things like creating a sense of urgency, creating and communicating the vision, empowering others to act, and creating short-term wins among others. Managing change can be made easier if leaders keep in mind that their workforce needs to be clear on the vision of the organization so there will not be any confusion. The employees need to have the right skills so as to minimize anxiety, along with the proper incentives. They need to have the resources needed to achieve the change in order to minimize frustration, and there should be a game plan so as to reduce false starts.

3

Technology's Impact

*The only sustainable competitive advantage is an organization's ability to
learn faster than the competition.*

—Peter Senge, (The Fifth Discipline, 2010)

Fortune 500 CEOs consider one of their biggest challenge today is "the rapid pace of technological change" (Murray, 2016). Technology is continuing to increase its creativity, change, and capability for greater connectivity, making globalization that much more relevant. It took the radio 38 years to reach 50 million users, the TV 13 years, the Internet 4 years (Figure 3.1).

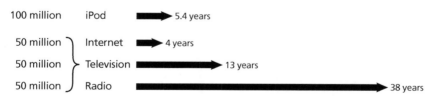

Figure 3.1   Technology timeline.

The Perfect Human Capital Storm, pages 9–14
9

For mobile devices it took more than 5 years to reach 100 million. In the beginning of the 1900s, the rich were involved in the automobile industry; today, a large majority of these working rich have transitioned and are now involved in the information technology (IT) industry.

An interesting visual (Figure 3.2) shows how it is estimated that every minute, Netflix subscribers stream over 77,000 hours of video, there are over 4,300 unique visitors to Amazon, and Apple users download 51,000 apps, while Facebook users "like" over 4 million posts (James, 2015).

Other research into the typical Internet minute estimates that there are 6 million Facebook views, more than 2 million Google searches, more than a million YouTube views, 300 hours of videos uploaded, more than 100 new LinkedIn signups, and more than 47,000 app downloads (Bhargava, 2014). This is expected to grow exponentially, taking into consideration places like South Korea where every home has been connected to the Internet, at one gigabyte per second, since 2012. It is estimated that someone in South Africa today has more access to communication and information than Reagan or Clinton did when they were president of the United States (Diamardis & Kotler, 2012). Others have highlighted that technology will enable humanity to live forever (Grossman, 2011).

It has been highlighted that 65% of CEOs see the increasing pace of technological change and 58% of CEOs see cybersecurity as two of the biggest challenges facing organizations in the 21st century (Murray, 2016). These are just examples of the exponential growth and impact of the Internet. The dramatically changing pace of technology has given rise to the knowledge economy, the digital workplace, the use of mobile technology, a culture of connectivity, a larger virtual workforce of telecommuters, and social connections and learning.

There are now businesses, opportunities, and terms that did not exist 10 or even 5 years ago. Terms like *texting* and *Twitter* did not exist in the year 2000. Today, there are concepts like *get a designated texter*. Recently BiblioTech, a library without physical books, was opened in Texas. The $2.4 million project, supported and led by Bexar County Judge Nelson Wolff, utilizes only technology (http://bexarbibliotech.org). Figure 3.3 is a visual related to this library.

What baby boomer would have imagined a library without books, but instead with all of the readings online or available through technology only. This just accentuates how times continue to change from what most of us have grown up with.

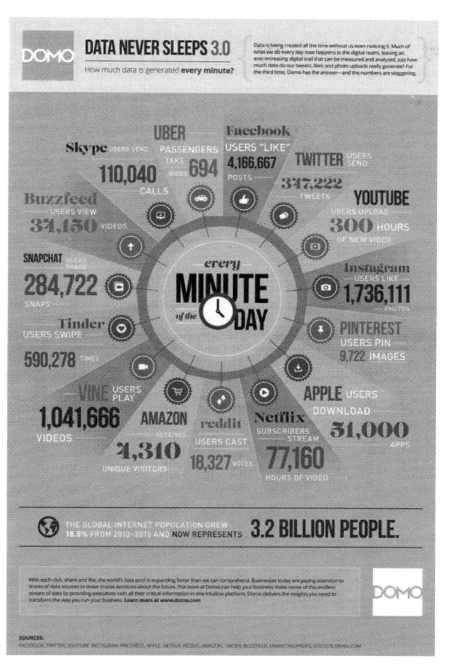

Figure 3.2 Data Never Sleeps 3.0

Figure 3.3 Visual of a bookless library.

It is estimated that there will be a $38 billion annual revenue generated by 2015 in smartphone and tablet apps. In 2010, there were more than $1.6 billion worth of mobile device purchases. Today, more people in the United States browse the web from their tablets than from their desktops (Frank, Roehrig, & Pring, 2014). In 2015 it was estimated that tablet sales would overtake desktop sales, and they did. In the early 2000s, *cybersecurity* was a term not heard by many.

Throughout all of this, a new term and framework emerged within the IT world in our everyday experience for safekeeping our information known as the cloud. The human cloud that is setting up what will enable our jobs to change in dramatic ways and will enable a flexible working environment as this disruptive technology takes hold (Garcia, 2015). This just enables the continuation of the changing workplace. There is the expansion of artificial intelligence (AI). A McKinesy Global Institute study highlighted that this area can potentially have a $14 trillion to $33 trillion impact and could transform society and our workplace experience to a larger scale faster than the Industrial Revolution ever did (The Economist, 2016).

This changing workplace will include a virtual workplace that will continue to grow and evolve. This will create opportunities and challenges for organizations, leaders, and HR departments regarding selection, development, retention, workplace dynamics, and organizational culture. In particular, on-going development will be key for the success of organizations and their workforce. Technology will enable workers to work differently and have to learn new skills with these changing technologies. Companies that maximize the learning and development opportunities that this evolving technology will create, will in turn enable a more engaged workforce, particularly their increasing Millennial workforce.

Recently, a research paper looked into the computerization of jobs. The authors found that an estimated 47% of U.S. employment is at risk of being computerized over the next decade or two (Frey & Osborne, 2013). This has a series of implications for organizations, the educational system, and the future of work overall. The educational system will need to prepare the future workforce. Organizations will need to increase on-going workforce development and ensure the their processes support the changing work.

Another way to view this is that technology is increasingly dominating both the economy and society. This is supported by the influx of all the technologically flavored movies, such as *Eagle Eye*, *Avatar*, and *Minority Report* just to name a few. This is further supported by the increasingly evolving technology in our everyday lives regarding advances in things like self-driving vehicles, smartphones, tablets, drones, artificial intelligence, and cybersecurity.

This was highlighted by Thomas Friedman on TV during the 2012 presidential race . He mentioned that when he wrote *The World is Flat*,

> Facebook didn't exist (or at least for most Americans), Twitter was a sound, the cloud was in the sky, 4G was a parking space, LinkedIn was a prison, applications were what you sent to college, and for most people Skype was a typo. This all changed in just the last seven years. What it has done is taken the world from connected to hyperconnected. (Friedman, 2011)

It has also changed how we work in ways that we would never have imagined back in 2000. It has raised the bar globally for competition. The way we work now has raised the level of the workforce needed to operate in the 21st century more than we ever thought possible. It has challenged how we educate (more to come on this later), how we work and collaborate, and who is now part of our team (the world—not just the person down the hall, rather the person down the virtual hall, regardless of where they are).

The 21st century organization will need to be smart, agile, and proactively ahead of its competitors in integrating mobile, social, cloud, and analytic technologies in order to reinvent itself through people, processes, and technologies (Frank et al., 2014).

So What Can an Organization Do?

The following are some considerations and recommendations.

Technology will continue to evolve. The challenge will be how organizations will integrate IT into the fabric of their organizational changes and strategies. More importantly, organizations will need to utilize the changing technology for more effective, productive, and efficient work that helps their organization outperform the competition. Organizations will have to assess how they use it to gain a competitive advantage.

Organizations—in particular, their leadership teams—will need to create a culture whereby technology is just one enabler of their strategy and not the silver bullet that will solve all of their challenges. While creating this culture, they must ensure that protection—in particular, cybersecurity—is at the forefront of their employees' minds as they embark toward making changes.

Ongoing development will need to be part of the organization's strategy; every iteration of change in technology will mean ongoing learning. In addition, organizations should ensure there is ongoing change management, because every piece of newly introduced technology will enable process, structural, and alignment changes.

4

Education

No one said that earning a living in the 21st century is going to require less education. It's going to require more.

—Edward E. Gordon
Future Jobs: Solving the Employment and Skills Crisis, 2013

While technology is playing more of a key role on the global workforce stage, the United States has an interesting challenge and opportunity in this area. This is particularly so because science, technology, engineering, and math (STEM) are areas that the United States are falling behind in globally. This appears to be more like the world is becoming leveled or balanced, and others are catching up (Augustine, 2008).

Presently the United States ranks 24th out of 50 countries in applying math concepts to real world problems. In the United States, 15% of undergraduates are in science and engineering fields compared with 38% in South Korea, 50% in China, and 67% in Singapore. The United States presently ranks 5th in the world in terms of how many people receive a college education with Russia, Canada, and Japan filling the top three spots (Frohlich, 2014).

The Perfect Human Capital Storm, pages 15–20
Copyright © 2017 by Information Age Publishing
15

In a sense, the United States is ceding its scientific and technical leadership. While this might be a fact, the interpersonal skills of empathy, creativity, and building relationships are increasingly becoming more important for the future workforce and organizations (Colvin, 2015). These changes are also taking place during a time when there is an increase in minorities, yet only close to 60% of these minorities have completed high school, 12% have completed bachelor's degrees, and 10% completed graduate degrees. A college education is becoming more what a high school education use to be (Rodriguez, 2007). This has recently begun to change some due to the tough economic times. Now, more minorities—particularly Latinos—are entering college due to limited and fewer educational employment opportunities.

While the United States works through its educational challenges, China and India are aggressively competing (Figure 4.1) to be part of the expanding educated workforce in the world, particularly in the STEM arena.

However they also have challenges. China and India have aging populations, and both do not have enough of an educated workforce for tomorrow's high-level workplace needs. What has arisen is that while these countries have educated many in their newly minted higher educational

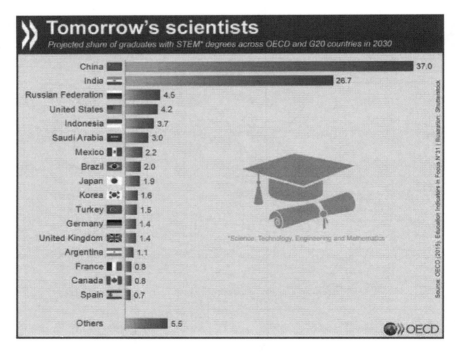

Figure 4.1 Projected scientists across OECD.

institutions, many of their graduates are coming up short when it comes to meeting minimum workplace requirements. It seems that at least in India, some of their diplomas might not be credible due to some recent challenges on the quality or validity of the education (Oneindia, 2016).

The United States, along with China and India, need to focus on rebuilding their education-to-employment systems for the masses in order to be competitive (Gordon, 2013). While the United States has the highest proportion of high school graduates entering college, it still has the lowest percentage of students completing their degrees. Due to these challenges, organizations are being forced to evolve from focusing on talent management to focusing on talent creation.

This will be particularly important since U.S. higher educational institutions continue to be where the world wants to come to get educated. The new American dream for Chinese parents, who at one time wanted to attend a U.S. college but could not, is to send their kids, who make up 21% of all international students and contribute an estimated $25 billion to the U.S. economy (Gordon, 2012). The problem with this is that they are being incentivized to return to China, despite the fact that we could use them here.

In addition, there are those who came here to get an education and overstayed their educational visas. Now they are here illegally. We have an opportunity to fix the broken system and keep them here to capitalize on the workforce shortage in the STEM fields. This is occurring while organizations in the United States will need an additional 3 million college-educated employees, a 16% increase, to meet the workforce demands of 2018.

Today, getting a college education is the equivalent of getting a lifetime debt, due to the increasing cost. Coupled with this are politicians who continue to cut education funding, which in turn makes it increasingly difficult to get a higher education. What this country needs in order to compete on the global stage is a more cost-effective education for all.

The following numbers should provide some reasons why education is a lifetime investment. Today, a high school dropout on average can expect to make approximately $18,000 per year; someone with a high school education can make more than $30,000; someone with a bachelor's degree can make $75,000; and someone with a graduate degree can make more than $100,000 a year (Locsin, 2014). Figure 4.2 shows the lifetime potential based on an individual's educational level. These obviously provide varied lifetime returns and opportunities. It's the difference between getting a job after school and getting a career.

So the questions are, what does an individual want, and what is he or she willing to do to make a difference in their lifetime earning capability?

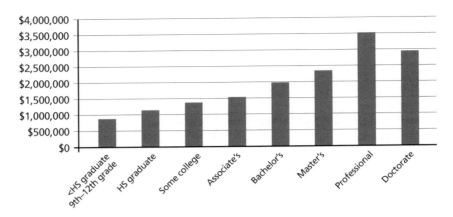

Figure 4.2 Lifetime earnings.

Of course, there are those who dropped out of college and pursued their dreams like Bill Gates, Steve Jobs, and Mark Zuckerberg among others. But we'd also have to admit that these are the exceptions, and the likelihood of success without a college degree is low. What we have to accept is that individual choices about higher education add up to and affect how organizations can evolve, adapt, and grow. Less of an education is not going to be a better option for individuals, and for organizations in turn that will need a more educated workforce (Meachum, 2013).

Today, many employers are having a difficult time finding qualified college graduates to hire. In addition, more than a third of 2011 college grads did not demonstrate a large increase in cognitive gains over the years (Gordon, 2012). This should trouble future employers. In summary, those who are able to pursue a higher education can actually do very well for themselves financially and economically over their lifetime versus those who do not; this has implications for organizations, societies, and countries in the future (Morgan, 2014).

There is also an interesting challenge certain politicians are placing us in, especially when the four fastest growing industry sectors are health care, IT, aerospace, and manufacturing all industries that will need employees with more than a high school diploma, and an educated workforce and more employees as baby boomers continue to retire in growing numbers. These are the same politicians who claim they want to educate our American children and future workforce, but do not provide the funding needed by schools and would rather provide more tax breaks for corporations. This is contradictory since cutting education funding at the state level reduces the opportunities for these same organizations to gain an educated workforce. An educated workforce is our best hope (Gordon, 2013).

How countries and organizations proactively plan for these challenges and opportunities will make the difference in regards to competing globally. With onoging changing technologies and a necessary advanced thinking and creative workforce, countries and organizations that invest now will reap benefits in the long run. This will be a challenge in a society that tends to favor immediate satisfaction and focuses on the short term.

Organizations should consider increasingly and proactively engaging in partnering with our educational system and schools, especially in a time when our politicians will not address them. Organizations might even consider partnering with the Bill and Melinda Gates Foundation, which has now partnered with the Rand Corporation on how to create a more comprehensive and progressive educational framework for our educational system (Pane, Steiner, Baird, & Hamilton, 2015). This is something worth considering as a starting point from an educational perspective, because what organizations will need is a more educated workforce. In the end, this is an important imperative for all countries and societies, and in particular more important to organizations for their success and existence.

So What Can An Organization Do?

The following are some considerations and recommendations.

Organizations should look to partner, collaborate, and volunteer with their local schools. While I recognize that many large organizations already do this to some extent, it needs to occur in a more focused and deliberate manner. I believe organizations should engage with their local schools as early as primary school. They should provide financial aid for equipping the schools with the appropriate resources, which can include technology infrastructure, computers, and other means to help bring schools, particularly those in lower-income neighborhoods, into the 21st century. This will enable these schools to better equip children for their future careers.

Organizations should also enable and motivate their workforce to volunteer some of their time to mentor, motivate, and educate the children in these schools about possible careers in order to provide them a glimmer of hope for their future. Employees can contribute some hours a year to pay it forward by reaching back into the schools that need it the most so that these children can gain role models, dream of possible careers, and look toward a better future.

In addition, companies should have representatives on school boards, or in some other capacity, so they can represent the interest of their organization's future workforce needs. Schools can ensure their curriculums are taking these needs into consideration as they educate their pupils. This should begin in primary school.

While I know that some might say educational choices should be left to the educational professionals, I believe most will agree that our educational system needs to be revisited and reframed for the needs of the 21st century workforce. Organizations cannot and should not sit idly by waiting for the educational system to continue to pump out an undereducated workforce. If organizations are the customers of what the educational system puts out, then a better collaborative partnership needs to be formed so that present and future needs are better met with a well-prepared workforce.

The educational system as an industry should reassess how it presently educates and look at reinventing the educational framework it uses to educate the future workforce. It might consider a paradigm shift (Robinson, 2010).

5

Society is Aging

Aging is not lost youth, but a new stage of opportunity and strength.
—Betty Friedan, BrainyQuote, 2006

Society is aging, and this is not just in the United States or just in one industry. In the year 2000, only a few countries had a population with more than 20% of residents age 6 or older. These were primarily European countries. Presently this percentage is growing and is expected to grow by 2025 with only Latin America (particularly Mexico), India, and Africa maintaining a younger society and in turn workforce. This in itself demonstrates that not only the United States but the world in general is aging (Strack, 2014). This creates interesting challenges and opportunities not only for organizations but also for countries. How do the underdeveloped countries create infrastructure, processes, and opportunities in order to capitalize on their large but unprepared and underdeveloped young workforce?

From a societal workplace perspective, the number 2.1 is a number that countries and organizations alike are going to become all too familiar with in the coming years. The reason for this is that this number represents the

The Perfect Human Capital Storm, pages 21–25
Copyright © 2017 by Information Age Publishing
All rights of reproduction in any form reserved.

| TABLE 5.1 Workforce Replacement Rate ||
Country	Replacement Rate
Spain	1.1
Germany	1.4
Japan	1.3
China	1.4
U.S.	2.0
India	2.8
Mexico	2.8

workforce replacement rate or what it will take organizations to backfill its workforce as society ages and labor shortages continue to increase around the globe (Shervani, 2009). The 2.1 takes into consideration immigration, emmigration, births, and deaths. The United States stands at 2.0, Mexico and India stand at 2.8, China is at 1.4, Japan is at 1.3, and Spain is at 1.1 (Table 5.1).

These numbers obviously present some interesting challenges for some of these countries. If a country's workforce replacement number is dramatically below 2.1, then what can it do to turn this around? The alarming issue for these countries is how to replace their exiting workforce.

Do they increase their recruitment efforts globally in order to attract potential employees from other countries? While this is definitely one option, it cannot be the only one because other countries also have a shortage. What will be their creative response to this shortage? Can automatizing their work help, and if so how much—and how soon can that be ready? And even if they upgrade by using automatization, who will they use to work in this new environment when most of these countries do not have enough of an educated or talented workforce to work in this new environment? This definitely presents challenges for these countries (Figure 5.1). This was further highlighted in the Ted Talk "The Workforce Crisis of 2030, and . . . *How to Start Solving It Now* by Rainer Strack emphasized that there will be an aging workforce with a skill shortage, particularly by 2030 (Strack, 2014).

All of this is occurring everywhere in the world, but it appears to be more obvious for the United States, where the baby boomers are beginning to retire or semiretire. Today's developed countries are leading the way into humanity's graying future. China, for one, has realized this (although perhaps not in time) and has recently relaxed its one-child law to allow those who have only one child to have two children. Furthermore, the average life expectancy in the 1900s was 47, and today it is 80.

GLOBAL WORKFORCE CRISIS

		Labor shortage/surplus in 2020	Labor shortage/surplus in 2030
EUROPE	🇫🇷 FRANCE	6%	-1%
	🇩🇪 GERMANY	-4%	-23%
	🇮🇹 ITALY	8%	-4%
	🇪🇸 SPAIN	17%	-3%
	🇬🇧 UK	6%	-1%
	🇷🇺 RUSSIA	-5%	-24%
AMERICAS	🇧🇷 BRAZIL	-7%	-33%
	🇨🇦 CANADA	3%	-11%
	🇲🇽 MEXICO	6%	-8%
	🇺🇸 USA	10%	4%
ASIA-PACIFIC	🇨🇳 CHINA	7%	-3%
	🇮🇳 INDIA	6%	1%
	🇮🇩 INDONESIA	5%	0%
	🇯🇵 JAPAN	3%	-2%
	🇰🇷 SOUTH KOREA	-6%	-26%

Figure 5.1 Global workforce crisis.

This means that not only will there be a brain drain or a loss of workforce knowledge and experience, but there will also be a workforce drain with a large retired population. How countries and organizations proactively prepare to address these challenges will be critical and imperative to their future.

Over the next 20 years in the United States, 80% of workforce growth will be due to those over the age of 50 (Nassar, Johnson, & Lichter, 2008). More than 70% expect to continue working after retirement. Increasingly more people are "working for a purpose," or working for something beyond a paycheck and for more personal meaning. While most of us are used to reading about the best employers to work for if you are a woman, a minority, or beginning your career, the American Association of Retired Persons (AARP) also has a best employer list.

The organizations on this list are competitive in the areas of employee development, health benefits, workforce age, alternative work arrangements, time off, retirement benefits, and pensions. At least three of these categories are relevant and applicable to employees of any age—employee development, health benefits, and alternative work arrangements.

What is presently happening is that for every two experienced workers leaving the workforce, only one relatively inexperienced worker joins it (Hesselbein & Goldsmith, 2009). This means that the future workforce is already born, finite, and shifting. How organizations adapt to this increasingly aging workforce will create global changes. This loss of an experienced workforce will become increasingly relevant as we continue to evolve as a global society. What will this mean for countries, organizations, and society in general? How will the organizations of today adapt to this aging workforce in the future? What will the next 20 or 30 years force countries and organizations to do in order to adapt to meet this potentially older society and workforce?

As society ages, there are business and social opportunities increasingly being created (Jackson, Howe, & Nakashima, 2011). For example, there is an increasing demand for the care of the aging population. In addition, there are more baby boomers who are not only raising their children but also caring for their parents. There are the increasing health care concerns of the aging population with illnesses such as Alzheimer's. Some countries, such as China, have not yet figured out how to address some illnesses, or are culturally uncomfortable addressing them. These changes create not only challenges, but also opportunities for part-time work for those getting close to retirement, and to increased knowledge-sharing opportunities between the newer/younger workers and older/experienced ones.

Earlier, there was the mention of the possible automatization of work. While this is a possible approach to handling the aging workforce and the workforce shortage, it will not serve as the silver bullet for organizations going forward. Not all work can be automatized as there will always be some form of manual work. Additionally, there will still be the need for higher-level, critical, problem solving, and analytical thinking to address problems and issues that we have not even thought of yet (Gordon, 2013). So while there are a lot of futuristic Hollywood movies of a possible future where technology will be the norm, this will not be the only alternative society that organizations will need to consider when addressing the future of work and the potential shortage of a workforce, particularly in regards to the workforce with limited education (more to come on this later).

Competition is increasing at a global level for the limited aging (and in turn decreasing), skilled, and/or educated workforce. It will be interesting to see how organizations adapt to their new real world order and new normal of a limited skilled workforce. While some futurists say water will be our future shortage, there is also the belief that a limited, highly sought after skilled, and/or educated demographic will be our future shortage. I hope I'm wrong.

So What Can An Organization Do?

For starters, an organization should create an environment, a culture, and practices where knowledge is shared. Knowledge management and sharing are not something that most organizations do, or do well. As baby boomers get ready to retire, organizations should consider establishing systems, processes, and practices enabled by reward and accountability so employees are motivated to capture and share their knowledge. In the same vein, the younger generation should be enabled, held accountable, and rewarded not only for learning from the older generations, but also for sharing what they know.

Creating an environment that allows everyone to collaborate, learn, and share can enable an organization to produce an exciting and vibrant culture. It can help position an organization to outperform its competition by establishing a learning environment. An organization that is constantly reinventing itself by sharing knowledge and information is positioning itself for the future by enabling its future workforce.

In addition to creating an engaging, sharing, and collaborative environment, the organization should implement activities that enable it to thrive by creating practices and processes that serve what motivates different generations in the organization. This ensures that it provides ongoing development specific to the generations and caters to the evolving organizational needs. In spite of all of this technology talk, it is the interpersonal, people skills like teaming, cultural sensitivity, and colloboration among others that the future workforce will need (Colvin, 2015).

Another idea an organization should consider is an HR policy that enables older, soon-to-be-retired employees to work through some form of part-time arrangement. This allows those who might not immediately retire a creative opportunity to continue to contribute, minimizing an organization's pain of exiting a valuable portion of their workforce.

There are other ideas I'm sure an organization can develop and use to maximize the four (soon to be five) generations in the workforce. It's a matter of enabling a creative and innovative organizational workforce to work on it.

6

The Changing U.S. Demographics

Strength lies in differences, not in similarities.
—Stephen Covey, BrainyQuotes, 2014

The United States is demographically and dramatically changing. As recently as 2008, minority children were outnumbering White children in one out of six counties across the country. In some counties, minority kids comprised more than 50% (Nassar et al., 2009). This is the largest growing portion of our society, and it is estimated that there are 52 million Latinos in the United States. It is also estimated that by 2015 and 2017, Latinos will make up the largest chunk of entrants into the workforce segment in California and the workplace in general (Bordas, 2013). By 2050, the Latino population is projected to represent more than half of the U.S. workforce (Nassar et al., 2009). This is only one sign of the changing demographic times, where over the last 100 years the majority immigrants have gone from traditionally European to now Mexican (Pew Research, 2015).

The United States currently hosts the largest number of Latinos outside of Mexico, home to 108 million Latinos (Rodriguez, 2007). This includes

The Perfect Human Capital Storm, pages 27–34
Copyright © 2017 by Information Age Publishing
All rights of reproduction in any form reserved.

23 other Latin American countries. There are more Latinos in the United States than there are Canadians in Canada or Spaniards in Spain. The United States has the world's second-largest Spanish-speaking population only after Mexico. The immigrants coming to the United States today are different from those that arrived here a hundred years ago. See Figure 6.1.

Of the 52 million Latinos in the United States, 10 million to 12 million are estimated to be here illegally. Ironically, what is keeping America younger and competitive in the aging global environment is immigration, the very issue that created this country yet separates Americans. There are differing opinions on how to turn the 10 million to 12 million illegal immigrants into an active workforce, which is something that economists have indicated would positively affect the American economy.

While many uninformed Americans believe that these illegal immigrants come to the United States by illegally crossing the Rio Grande, the reality is that almost half of those here illegally actually came here on visas from around the world and have overstayed them, and most are not from Mexico (Robbins, 2006). Some of them have the very skills that this country's workforce needs. This is why organizations such as those in Silicon Valley are hoping for some sort of resolution so that we can take advantage of a highly skilled portion of this illegal workforce in the United States, where there is a shortage of highly skilled workers. Yet many believe, due to misinformation and possibly racism, that the undocumented workers here are all migrant workers from Mexico.

The shortage is not helped by the fact that we do not have enough American college students pursuing science, technology, engineering, and math (STEM) degrees (Augustine et al., 2008). What is beginning to occur is that countries like China and India are creating incentives for those who live abroad—for example, in the United States—to come back to work in their countries since they too are dealing with an aging society and the lack of an educated workforce.

It is estimated that of the 10 million to 12 million illegal immigrants in the United States, more than 50% are from Mexico, but this has been declining as more return to their native home (Krugstad,Passel, & Cohn, 2016). Most would agree that they did not come here to go to Disneyland, to take jobs away from our American workforce, or live off of the government. They instead currently serve primarily as the United States migrant laborers.

There is an opportunity here to capitalize on this workforce. After all, how many Americans want to work on our farms as day laborers, especially for less than minimum wage and to perform these very physical jobs? As it

Note: Countries are defined by their modern-day boundaries, which may be different from their historical boundaries. Russia and the former USSR countries are combined in this analysis, even though the Soviet Union was only in existence between 1922 and 1991. Birthplace is self-reported by respondents. Arizona and New Mexico became states in 1912. Alaska and Hawaii became states in 1959. Sample size in North Carolina is too small to analyze in 1910.
Source: Based on Pew Research Center tabulations of of 2009-2011 American Community Surveys and 1910 Census, IPUMS.

Figure 6.1 Where each state's largest immigrant population was born (Top nation of origin by state).

is today, we have minimum-wage earners working at Walmart, McDonald's, Burger King, and others, who are fighting to raise their minimum wages.

While illegal immigration is wrong, we should look to minimize the politicization of it and work for something that benefits all. There should be a comprehensive plan that addresses those who have lived here for some time, and address the issue that organizations need them here to do a job that most Americans will probably not do, especially at the low wages.

The other point that seems to get most organizations' attention is the buying power of the Latino community in the United States, which was estimated at more than $1 trillion in 2010 and is expected to reach $1.7 trillion by 2020. This purchasing power is estimated to be larger than the entire economies of all but the top 15 countries (out of 194) in the world (Rodriguez, 2008). Hopefully this provides you a better understanding as to why there are ATMs that have both English and Spanish as options to choose from when completing a transaction. In addition, many organizations offer automated phone service in English or Spanish. This is not happening just to be politically correct. This is a reflection of the economic power and impact of this demographic group.

Add to this that in comparing (Figure 6.2) the 52 million Latino demographic to the BRIC countries (Brazil, Russia, India, and China), while they are each much larger population wise from a GDP perspective, the U.S. Latino demographic is at $31,000 plus; the next closest is $11,000. From a year-over-year growth perspective, the U.S. Latino demographic is at 3.2%, while the next closest is India at 1.4% (Cartegena, 2013).

In addition, there are currently 22 cities where minorities are the new majority, and it is estimated that by 2017 Latinos will make up the majority of the entrants into the workforce. There are some additional points to keep in mind regarding the interesting shift in age when it comes to these different demographics in our country. For starters, the average age of Latinos in this country is 27-years-old, while for Anglos it is 40. There are the one-to-one and one-to-eight ratios that basically say that for every Anglo who dies, one is born; for every Latino who dies, eight are born (Rodriguez, 2008). Rodriguez goes on to point out that the Latino group brings a larger focus to the belief in Catholicism (or at least Christianity), as they have historically placed importance on family, humility, respect for leaders, and stability. As a matter of fact, it is seen as the growth or at least stability of the Catholic Church; in Europe and the United States the Catholic numbers are either stable or declining, while Catholicism continues to grow in Latin America and among Latinos in the United States. Their worldview

A Country Within a Country

	Brazil	Russia	India	China	U.S. Hispanics
Total Population (in millions)[1,2]	197.5	142.5	1,189.1	1,336.7	52
GDP (current dollars)[3,4]	$2.28T	$2.38T	$4.46T	$11.29T	$1.1T
GDP per capita (PPP)[3,4]	$11,600	$16,700	$3,700	$8,400	$31,135*
YOY Pop Growth	0.9%	–0.1%	1.4%	0.5%	3.2%**

Figure 6.2 Hispanic per capita income vs. BRIC countries.

Source: 1) U.S. Census Bureau International Database Division. Population Estimates for 2011; 2) U.S. Census Bureau. 2011 Population Estimates. Released May, 2012; 3) CIA Fact Book. Country rankings based on 2011 Estimates; 4) IHS Global Insight–2010 Hispanic Market Monitor. Based on 2011 Estimates.
* Based on average Hispanic household income in 2010.
** Based on U.S. Hispanic population growth from April 1, 2010 to July 1, 2011. Country population growth based on % growth in total population by country 2010 vs. 2011.

is rooted in family, spirituality, and a holistic view of past, present, and future. This has implications for organizations from a diversity and inclusion perspective.

It will also be interesting to see how this moral compass, religious preference, and cultural perspective will impact American corporations. These corporations have typically had a cultural makeup of an Anglo-capitalistic way of controlling one's destiny, speaking and bragging about one's strengths, successes, and a mentality of "look what I bring to the organization." Latinos have traditionally been raised to demonstrate humility, a focus on family, respect, and faith in God. This mindset results in interesting challenges and opportunities for organizational talent acquisition, management, development, and diversity, both from an employee and customer point of view. If they come into the workforce with a built-in loyalty mindset, and respect for their organization and leader, then there is an opportunity for leaders to maximize this mindset and create an engaged and growing workforce.

The difficulty facing this group is that while it makes up almost one-sixth of the U.S. population, its members traditionally have not pursued a higher education, which is, and will continue to be needed in the workplace in the 21st century. It is estimated that almost 70% of college-age Latinos entered college in 2013, up from 40% in 2000; yet only 1 in 10 will actually complete college (Univision, 2013). This is important because more jobs will require more than just a high school education. In addition, the Millennials, who are presently seen as the growing portion of the workforce, are mostly Latino (estimated at 44%) and have experienced discrimination. This is particularly important to note, because in a recent study it was found that those who were considered different (Latinos, African Americans, and women) might have a more difficult time getting through a hiring interview (Burrell, 2016).

The future workplace will need a higher level of thought process, problem solving, and critical thinking. Organizations will need to create an engaging and inclusive workplace that enables this type of behavior. It is imperative that this occurs so that organizations can achieve success and in order to stay competitive in the 21st century.

By 2020, nearly three-fourths of the predicted growth in the labor market will be due to Latinos (Erickson, 2014). This is a powerful statement and a wake-up call for organizations and their future workforces. As this demographic change continues, it will create interesting dynamics when it comes to the terms *minority* and *majority* and will have lasting implications on how organizations engage and expect supervisors to lead an increasingly diverse workforce. This will have implications for the traditional and legal EEO/AAP practices in U.S. organizations today. It will have implications for team dynamics, something seen as critical for the future of work (Bersin, 2016a). The traditional paradigm of the terms minority and majority are shifting as you read this book. This topic was recently in the news as it is estimated that by 2050, what we know today as minority and majority will shift.

To complicate this further, we should consider what it means to be Latino in the United States with 27 different nationalities and various migration patterns with different cuisines and social mores (Bordas, 2013). Being a first- or second-generation American further adds to the complexities of English, Spanish, or Spanglish (a combination of English and Spanish) languages. Organizations cannot and should not just brand all Latinos as the same because they fall under this particular demographic.

All of this begs the question of how organizations will either reactively or proactively engage in capitalizing on this demographic shift. How will they continue to market to Latinos? More importantly, how will they integrate them as part of their organizational leadership teams?

Our future will be different. This is not the only minority group growing that will make America more diverse. It is estimated that by 2065 Asians will outnumber Latinos in the United States (Cohn, 2015). We will need to integrate the upcoming and changing workforce. Organizations will need to adapt in order to attract, develop, and retain this diverse workforce. Diversity is truly becoming a competitive advantage with increasing complexity. How the United States and organizations address the increasing and changing demographics is still an open-ended question, but there are opportunities. With one group aging, primarily the traditional Anglo baby boomers, increasing diversity will be needed.

Organizations that truly create a welcoming, engaging, and inclusive environment that sees diversity as a strategic advantage will be in a better position. Since the growing demographic now is Latinos, organizations should look to promote qualified Latinos to leadership positions that not only will serve to add to their diverse leadership teams, but also have increased role models in their organizations.

So What Can an Organization Do?

Organizations not only need to attract this large workforce, but they also need to develop and grow it. Organizations need to make them part of their future leadership team, especially with the increasing value of diversity for organizations, particularly in the United States. Recruiting Latinos to join organizations will not be enough. They will need to ensure they are developing and promoting this diverse group into leadership to bring a variety of perspectives to the leadership table.

The following are some considerations and recommendations.

Organizations should look to partner, collaborate, and volunteer with their local communities and schools. As the demographics of this country continue to change, the "browning of America," as I once heard a news reporter call it, will be a larger segment of the workforce.

Organizations should look to partner with the educational system to come up with some creative strategies so there are incentives for this growing demographic to fill the need of highly skilled workers. This group will replace the outgoing and retiring baby boomers. There should be partnerships with organizations and their local communities and schools to educate this population as to the increasing educational needs and avenues to meet these needs so they can become part of the future workforce.

Executives need to create comprehensive talent acquisition, mentoring, leadership development, and talent management programs that capitalize on maximizing the benefits of this diverse talent base. They need to ensure their programs truly do reach out to this group so that Latinos can be further integrated into the future of organizations through a proactive leadership and employee development effort—an effort that is visible both within the organization and externally to the growing diverse customer base, maximizes the richness of the diversity of this group, and capitalizes on it as a business strategy.

7

Four Generations in the Workplace (Soon to Be Five)

If you want happiness for a lifetime, help the next generation.
—Chinese Proverb, Thinkexist.com, 2017

Presently in the United States, we have the older workers known as veterans, aged 61 and older, who make up 5% of the workforce; the baby boomers, aged 43 to 60, who make up 45% of the workforce; the Generation Xers, aged 30 to 42, who make up 40% the workforce; and the Millennials, or Net Generation, aged 29 or younger, who make up 10%. In addition, there are some that say we'll actually have a fifth generation, known as Gen 2020, which will include those born after 1997 (Meister & Willyerd, 2010).

Two of these generations seem to have a greater impact on organizations—the Millennials and baby boomers. Some would argue that these two groups have completely opposite philosophies, goals, and work ethics, while others argue that they are not that different at all. The bottom line is that organizations need to capitalize on the diversity of their workforce, regardless of their generational makeup and perspective.

The Perfect Human Capital Storm, pages 35–38
Copyright © 2017 by Information Age Publishing
All rights of reproduction in any form reserved.

The Net Generation (aka the Millennials) is presently having and will continue to have a dramatic impact on the workplace (Tapscott, 2008). Members prefer to work collaboratively with a need for freedom. They seem to place a greater emphasis on family relationships, citizen engagement, worldliness, corporate integrity and openness, innovation, and efficiency and fun at work.

Millennials have been labeled impatient, technologically savvy, self-absorbed, and just plain spoiled (some blame their helicopter—a.k.a., baby boomer—parents). Not surprisingly, they see themselves as completely different then the perception (or stereotypes) of them. The Millennials are actually expected to make up 50% of the workforce by 2020 and 75% of the workforce by 2025 (Morgan, 2016).

The different perspective of this generation could not be more obvious than in a recent study (O'Donnell, 2013) of HR professionals. The study found that 14% of HR professionals perceived this generation to be less people savvy, while 65% of Millennials perceived themselves as more people savvy. Eighty-six percent of HR professionals felt this generation was more tech savvy, while only 35% this group rated themselves this way. Eighty-two percent of Millennials considered themselves loyal, compared with only 1% of HR that saw them this way. Finally, 86% of Millennials considered themselves to be hard workers, while only 11% of HR professionals believed this. This generation is expected to make up 50% of the global workforce by 2020.

In reality, Millennials are not that different than their baby boomer parents, who when they were growing up rebelled against "the establishment." They want to make a positive difference, do work they enjoy, and have a work–life balance (Pfau, 2016). Growing up, they have watched their baby boomer parents get downsized, laid off, reorganized, stressed out, and just overworked. Hopefully, they'll learn something from those situations and make a difference instead of repeat their parents' experiences.

This younger generation will have plenty of opportunities and challenges within their organizations and in society in general. Some opportunities will be to change the culture of constant downsizing, decrease stress due to overload, create a truly engaged workplace, and possess more of a global view in regards to technological support and integration.

A second generation that is still having an impact is the baby boomer generation. They are getting closer to retirement (the first wave has started to retire already), and with this they will have the opportunity to transfer knowledge to upcoming generations. This is important because for every two experienced and knowledgeable baby boomers who retire, there is one inexperienced employee joining the workforce (Xavier, 2009).

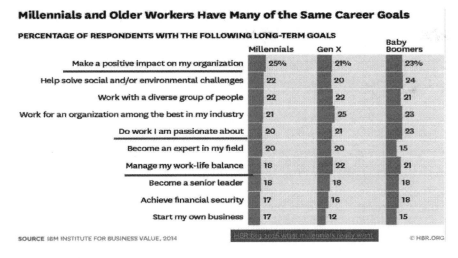

Millennials and Older Workers Have Many of the Same Career Goals

PERCENTAGE OF RESPONDENTS WITH THE FOLLOWING LONG-TERM GOALS

	Millennials	Gen X	Baby Boomers
Make a positive impact on my organization	25%	21%	23%
Help solve social and/or environmental challenges	22	20	24
Work with a diverse group of people	22	22	21
Work for an organization among the best in my industry	21	25	23
Do work I am passionate about	20	21	23
Become an expert in my field	20	20	15
Manage my work-life balance	18	22	21
Become a senior leader	18	18	18
Achieve financial security	17	16	18
Start my own business	17	12	15

SOURCE IBM INSTITUTE FOR BUSINESS VALUE, 2014   HBR.org 2016 what millennials really want   © HBR.ORG

Figure 7.1   Millennials and older workers career goals similarities.

They have seen quite a bit to a certain extent: wars that they thought were wrong, layoffs, downsizing, growth, the establishment of the middle class, financial success (and sometimes failure), credit cards and debt, and the boom and drought of real estate as their homes went up and down in price. They've seen the creation of the Internet, the cell phone evolution through the technology revolution, other countries competing with the superpower in regards to an educated workforce, four generations in the workplace, diversity, and changing U.S. demographics (Hesselbein & Goldsmith, 2009). They've watched their children journey through things they never did. They've experienced the ups and downs of life, including the tragedy that took place on 9/11. They've seen their 12-inch TVs increase to 50 and 60 inches and beyond with something now known as HDTV. They are able to enjoy movies on Netflix and online from the comfort of their homes. They've been exposed to laws that they would have never imagined when they were in their 20s, like "don't text and drive." In summary, they've seen things they never even imagined when they were in their teens.

Organizations will be challenged and have opportunities to integrate this workforce in a way that can enable them to outperform the competition (Hay, 2012). Organizations will need to proactively address how to capitalize on this new and changing workforce. How organizations and leaders integrate this changing workforce can provide a competitive advantage for them. How organizations capitalize on this diverse workforce (from an age perspective) will enable them to differentiate themselves from their competitors. However, if this varied aging workforce is not managed correctly, it can serve as a major loss for organizations, not only from a worker perspective but also from a customer perspective.

In the end, the proactive pursuit of engaging their diverse workforce will serve as a catalyst for their future success and existence.

So What Can an Organization Do?

The following are some considerations and recommendations.

Organizations should create educational programs that will help all of these generations in the workforce understand each other better, learn what motivates each group and discover how to better work together, and help everyone understand that while the different generations bring different perspectives and possibly even different values, it can be a good thing.

The leadership of the organization should also be expected to attend some form of education on the diversity of these generations in the workforce and learn how to capitalize on their differences and strengths. Leadership should be expected to learn how to create effective team dynamics through the strength of the diversity of the different generations in the workplace. There should also be both accountability measures and rewards from the executives through all ranks of leadership through annual incentives so that the leadership team ensures the workforce understands what is expected, is supported, and is rewarded when it comes to a diverse workforce.

There should also be a systemic and focused effort to ensure that teams formed include all generations when possible in order to maximize the diversity, creativity, and innovative ideas that different generations can bring to organizational challenges and opportunities.

In a recent study by Center for Creative Leadership (CCL) of 128 senior-level executives, 86% felt it was "extremely important" that employees colloborate across boundaries, yet only 7% believed they are effective (Yip, Ernst, & Campbell, 2011). This gap presents a huge opportunity for an organization to create a culture and process that engages their workforce across generations.

8

Employee Engagement

> *The workforce of today has different expectations. They are looking for fair rewards,*
> *flexibility and engaging work. In essence they are looking to be treated as adults.*
> —Alison Maitland and Peter Thomson, *Future Work,* 2011

Employee engagement has become a term front and center in organizations with bottom-line implications in recent times. It is estimated that 11% of employees are highly engaged, while 13% are not, and 76% are sitting on the fence and up for grabs. It is estimated that employee disengagement costs organizations an estimated $450 billion to $550 billion dollars a year. In a recent organizational survey, 90% of respondents cited employee engagement being critical to their success, yet 75% indicated that they did not have a strategy to address this human capital issue (Hay, 2012).

When organizations address employee engagement positively, they reap benefits. A recent Gallup poll of more than one million employees found that those in the top 25% of engaged workers have some of the following characteristics: 65% lower turnover, 48% fewer safety incidents, 37% lower absenteeism, 21% higher productivity, and 10% higher customer metrics (Harter, Schmidt, Killham, & Agrawal, 2009).

The Perfect Human Capital Storm, pages 39–42
Copyright © 2017 by Information Age Publishing
All rights of reproduction in any form reserved.

Despite this, some organizations continue to rank and stack employees against each other and to administer layoffs. Layoffs have been shown over time to be bad for business. Pfeffer found that of 141 layoff announcements between 1979 and 1997, this incurred negative stock returns. An additional 1,445 organizational layoff efforts between 1990 and 1998 also negatively impacted stock market returns. In another study of 210 organizations, a variety of performance measures were followed only to find that while the initial year after layoffs was positive, it was not the following year. In addition, it has been found that 88% of downsizing organizations had a negative impact on morale (Pfeffer, 2010).

This strategy has continued to be used as a quick fix by organizations, even though it negatively impacts the bottom line. Layoffs tend to increase employee disengagement. In addition, they also impact the health of employees. Continuing to do the same thing yet expecting different results has not usually worked.

As if employee engagement was not an important and relevant topic in today's organizations, leadership continues to focus on their high-potential and low performers forgetting almost 80% of the workforce. Operating with this managerial mindset and focus will only minimize the impact and potential of an engaged workforce. One aspect is the commitment to the team, the job, and the organization. This leads in turn to discretionary effort and intent to stay or leave by increasing engagement and commitment (Corporate Leadership Council, 2004).

When this is addressed effectively, it can lead to higher total returns to shareholders (TRS). It has been noted that highly engaged employees lead to better business outcomes, loyal customers, and improved financial performance. Having more engaged employees tends to attract high-level employees and results in higher levels of employee productivity and less turnover. High employee engagement also leads to improved customer service and reduced safety incidents.

An additional benefit is that during difficult times, a highly engaged workforce positions the organization for success. In addition, externally changing factors have less of an impact on these organizations. In organizations with a highly engaged workforce, an interesting positive cycle occurs. In good times, engagement enables success and profits. In difficult times, an engaged workforce and environment drive up profits (Hay, 2012).

Another way to look at this is that engagement can be interpreted as "a way of being" for an organization. We still have a long way to go for organizations to embrace and proactively integrate engagement into the fabric of their business practices and culture. As an example, 50% of European multinational organizations currently address engagement, but it is increasing in importance and visibility (Harter et al., 2009). In order to be proactive in this area, it needs to come from the top of the organization as a business and strategic imperative.

This backdrop and increasingly supporting research only reinforces the crucial role that supervisors play in enabling employee engagement. Effective leader-employee relationships, regardless of whether the company is traditional or virtual, can lead to highly satisfied and engaged workers, which in turn leads to improved customer service and loyalty, which in turn translates to a positive bottom line (Mouriño-Ruiz, 2005).

Organizations in the 21st century will need to transition from top-down hierarchies to nimble organizations that can adapt and change quickly with open and transparent communications. This way everyone is in the know. They will or should consider evolving from the mindset of just competing for market share to creating new markets. There are plenty of organizations existing today that provide services that did not exist before the year 2000, including Netflix, Pandora, Amazon, Uber, and Facebook just to name a few.

In order to maximize their effect on employee engagement, leaders will need to evolve from an organization-centric mentality to one that is people centric. This involves a shift from an environment based on command and control to one based on networks and relationships. These changes and paradigm shifts will help those organizations that truly want to reinvent themselves and create an engaging workplace and great place to work. In essence, leaders should move from asking the questions How can I get the most out of my employees, to What can I do to help my employees be more effective and engaged? In asking that question, leaders should increasingly recognize their employees for doing a good job, which has turned out to be the number one item chosen by more than 200,000 respondents in a global job preference survey (Strack, 2014). So what can an organization do?

The following are some considerations and recommendations.

Organizations first need to reassess their layoff practices and philosophy. Will they continue to practice short-term fixes, which actually have negative financial and human capital returns? Will they actually continue to profess that they are "a great place to work" or our "employees are our greatest asset," while they continue to treat their employees as expendable items? As organizations and their leadership reflect on this, they will need to assess what type of organizational culture they have and aspire to have. Are they claiming one thing and showing another with their behavior?

The process begins with leadership. It requires organizations to transform into becoming a great place to work and not just an organization that says it is one. Ultimately, the culture of an organization is a reflection of the personalities of its leaders. This means that organizations will need to not only ensure they are developing leaders to ensure that their employees feel valued, developed, and appreciated, but also to maintain practices that support this belief. Layoffs might not be one of them.

Leaders should consider asking their employees what they believe constitutes an engaging environment. By asking, they can gain a lot of insight and increased buy-in as they roll out efforts to create an engaging workplace. They should also research best practices of those organizations that are seen as role models and best practices of having an engaged workforce. With this upcoming shortage due to the aging population, employee engagement will be a key human capital strategy in order to attract and retain a workforce.

Leadership will need to be armed with the proper skills through ongoing leadership education as to how to create an engaging workforce. They will need to be enlightened about what makes an engaging organizational culture and their key role in this effort. They will also need to be held accountable for supporting the professed engaged workforce and be rewarded for supporting the vision of creating a great place to work that leads to employee engagement.

9

Leadership Development

Management is doing things right; leadership is doing the right things.
—Peter F. Drucker, BrainyQuotes, 2017

Studies continue to demonstrate that the main reason employees leave organizations and/or remain disengaged is poor management and lack of leadership. Almost 80% of executives have cited the ability to develop leaders as one of the most important factors that will impact competitive advantage. In a recent study (Gentry, Eckert, Stawski, & Zhao, 2016), 56% of organizations indicated that the lack of leadership would impede organizational performance, and 31% said that the shortage of leaders would impact organizations in the next few years. Another bottom-line implication is that organizations with top-tier leadership have up to 10% higher 3-year total shareholder returns.

If one was to look for leadership books on Amazon, they would probably find more than 150,000 titles and an estimated 750 million hits on Google on the topic of leadership. Billions of dollars have been spent on leadership development programs. Yet in spite of this, the majority of

The Perfect Human Capital Storm, pages 43–46
Copyright © 2017 by Information Age Publishing
All rights of reproduction in any form reserved.

people in the workforce do not trust their senior management. According to David Rock, one of the reasons that organizations fail is that they tend to hire and promote generations of managers with robust analytical skills and poor social skills, not thinking it matters (Rock 2013).

This idea is reinforced by the fact that 89% of managers believe employees leave organizations for more money, while only 12% of employees believe this. In recent times, particularly in the difficult economic downturn, there still appears to be a disconnect between managers and employees. Eighty percent of managers believe employees are just glad to have a job, while only 53% of employees feel this way. This means the employees are just waiting for a change in employment opportunities before they move on to other opportunities. It has been estimated that 51% of the time when employees leave organizations, it is due to their managers (Branham, 2005). This can cost an organization 150% of an employee's salary.

The way a person in authority treats their employees leads to the impact of leader-employee relationships, and this in turn can impact the bottom line of an organization (Mouriño-Ruiz, 2005). How this is managed becomes increasingly relevant for the success of an organization. In a recent study, the Center for Creative Leadership (CCL) found that there were six common challenges across organizations, industries, and the globe that were related to human capital. Developing managerial effectiveness, inspiring others, developing employees, leading a team, managing change, and managing both internal and external stakeholders and politics (Gentry et al., 2016). While a challenge, this study highlights how these challenges are global and what organizations need to focus on so that if it addresses these proactively and positively, it can serve as a best practice, and role model for other organizations to emulate and strive for.

Leaders need to consider the comprehensiveness of their role. A recent *Inc.* magazine article, "Between Mars and Venus," highlighted the blend of male and female traits that effective leaders demonstrate. The author (Buchanan, 2013) makes the case that effective leaders demonstrate empathy, inclusiveness, vulnerability, generosity, humility, balance, and patience. As I've conducted hundreds of leadership workshops over the last almost 40 years, I have always asked for characteristics of effective leaders. A couple traits that continuously come up are communication and trust.

This provides organizations, especially leadership development professionals, an opportunity to ensure there is proper development for their leadership cadre. This is particularly imperative when there is an increasingly diverse workforce and at present a large population getting ready to move on to retirement.

These changing and challenging times are increasing the need for an engaging leader. This requires a transformational leadership approach in order to ensure employee engagement (Smikle, 2016). This is needed to accommodate the increasing demands being placed on leaders to deliver faster results and increase their interactions with others. This is occurring while only 32% of their organizations are satisfied with their senior leadership team (Garvin, 2013). This might be one of the reasons why some organizations like Gore and Zappos, among others, are trying out new models like going managerless (Morgan, 2014).

So What Can an Organization Do?

The following are some considerations and recommendations.

While there has been a large investment in leadership over time, this needs to continue in a different framework, comprehensively, with bottom-line implications on the investment. This last piece—investment—is key. Traditionally, leadership development along with learning and development has been seen as an expenditure. I believe organizations need to look at it instead as a long-term investment in the human capital of their organization.

Organizations need to assess what their leadership development is costing them and what the returns are. Is there high turnover, low morale, low employee engagement, and high employee relations complaints? As these issues surface, the revamped leadership development efforts need to address these questions and decide what sort of organizational culture the organizational leadership wants to embody.

The leadership development program needs to be comprehensive and integrated with an expected leadership philosophy: one that starts from a future leader, front leader type development, and works all the way up through the executive ranks. All leaders should be held accountable and rewarded for their development, for having to participate and model what is taught and expected.

Employees should be surveyed to assess their satisfaction with leadership values and educational frameworks. Leaders should have 360 assessments conducted every year as part of ongoing development. Leaders should also be expected to rotate through different areas of the company to further learn the business as well as learn more about the employee workforce that exists within their organization.

One area to consider is to make executive/leadership coaching a key part of the leadership development strategy. A recent study (Heinen &

Wiete, 2012) highlighted that the top reason for leaders to engage with a coach is to support leadership development. This also tends to enhance employee engagement.

10

So Now What?

*The significant problems we have cannot be solved at the same level
of thinking with which we created them.*
—Albert Einstein, Goodreads.com, 2017

For starters, organizations and their leadership need to realize that the organization of the 21st century will be different, and employee expectations are and will continue to change. The assessment has been that organizations have not kept up with the changes taking place, especially with the workforce's changing expectations (Mackey & Sisodia, 2014). Instead of top-down hierarchies, organizations will need to be nimble and transparent. Leaders will need to create people-centric, transparent, and trust-based organizations. What worked in the past will not help organizations in the future. It is because of this that leaders need to recognize that each of these trends on their own is difficult enough for organizations to address. Unfortunately, the reality of today is that they occur simultaneously. One key consideration to keep in mind is that due to the complexity, breadth, and depth of each of these trends, organizations will need to develop both a short- and long-term human capital strategy.

I believe this is not a human resources issues, but a management issue to resolve in order to reinvent their respective organizations. I do still believe this should be led by the chief human resources officer (CHRO) in partnership with a functional executive as co-sponsor. Initially, the CHRO can present to the CEO and executive staff a state of the organization in line with the trends that I've explained previously. Some of the recommendations should be for the organization to embark on a long-term human capital strategy that supports the overall organizational strategy based on the perfect storm trends and the implications for the organization. By the CHRO partnering with a functional executive co-sponsor and presenting and getting buy-in from the executive team, this is positioned not as an HR effort but as an organizational business imperative.

The way to make this happen is to charter a team of members at all levels who demonstrate high potential. These members should come from all parts of the organization and remain with the project for one year. The project will really be a multiyear effort, but every year new team members will be added. For this one-year rotation, this should become part of their objectives. This not only enables them to drive the strategy, but it also provides them exposure, networking, and overall insight into a long-term organizational strategic effort that is focused on the workforce improving employee engagement among others.

Teams are sponsored by an executive to address and develop recommendations and plans for each of the issues from an organizational perspective. There will be teams sponsored to address technology changes, multiple generations in the workplace, the aging workforce, changing demographics, employee engagement, leadership development, and organizational change. The plans the teams develop will need to have metrics and annual milestones so the organization can see the progress of this major organizational effort. By operating this way, this multifaceted human capital project becomes a holistic, comprehensive, systemic approach to addressing organizational issues.

Another way to consider approaching this is highlighted by Jacob Morgan in his *Future of Work* book. In it he highlights six things to consider utilizing when trying to implement some changes for these changing times: challenge assumptions based on these trends and of the present state and of the organization; create a team to help lead this change effort with an executive sponsor; define and articulate the future of work for the organization; communicate this often to the organization; experiment and empower employees to take action; and last, to implement broad-based change (Morgan, 2014). In essence, a systemic and holistic approach will be needed by leaders and their organizations in order to address the changes and trends taking place.

Change your thoughts and you change your world.
—Norman Vincent Peale, Brainyquote.com, 2017

Here are some considerations to keep in mind going forward:

1. For organizations, the implications of these trends are pretty simple and complicated at the same time. They are simple because leaders will need to remain proactively engaged as they address these changes and look to develop and implement strategies while prioritizing what will provide them with a competitive advantage. They are difficult because creating and implementing these strategies can be overwhelming. As we all know, change is not easy. The actions of leadership will be crucial for this process. Leaders will need to assess its brand and how this brand is impacting the organization.

2. Regardless of an organization's size, there are always challenges when trying to change. Employees are usually slow to respond for a variety of reasons. A small company sometimes has the challenge of limited resources and capital. Regardless of the challenges, organizations will need to develop a plan and work to implement it because inaction is not an option. If they do not adapt, the option could be to become the next Eckerd Drugs, Montgomery Ward, or Circuit City—extinct, like the dinosaurs.

3. Human capital strategy creation for organizations will need to include both faster and slower solutions in order to position them and their clients for success. Organizations and their leadership have not been as tolerable in the past of long-term solutions (even though that is exactly what is needed at times).

4. Some challenges are outside the control of organizations, such as the aging population and technological innovations. Therefore, organizations will need to focus on and prioritize what they can control and try to partner with external entities in order to develop a longer-term plan and solution for the bigger issues, such as education.

5. Another consideration is the growing diversity of the present and future workforce. An organization that learns how to maximize the advantage that this brings will better position itself for success. Enabling a workforce that truly represents an organization's customer base and can be sensitive to its needs will help add to its market share. Finally, consider adapting HR policies and practices to tap into a soon-to-be-retired workforce by offering part-time work or other creative options so as to not lose this workforce.

6. While technology is front and center in these changing times, at the end of it all organizations need to remember that it will still be all about the people. Organizations without people are just buildings. Leaders will need to support a network of teams, have a culture and purpose, accelerate learning, ensure there is career development, and be thinking of the employee experience (Bersin, 2016).

11

The Leader Factor

Tomorrow's companies will need to have the brains of a business school graduate and the heart of a social worker.

—Thomas Friedman
The World is Flat: A Brief History of the 21st Century, 2005

One of the most important factors to keep in mind is the important role of the leader in this ever-changing environment. As we know, employees don't leave organizations, they leave managers. A leader incorporates the following:

Learning organization
Executive sponsorship and support
Adapting and agile practices
Development
Engaged workforce
Recogntion and relationships

Learning will be a continuous need in organizations. The particular focus here is from a macro-organizational perspective. As technology continues to change at a rapid pace, the workforce becomes more diverse.

The Perfect Human Capital Storm, pages 51–57
Copyright © 2017 by Information Age Publishing

Traditional training of the past has been exactly that: part of the past. Organizational learning needs to be part of the fabric of the organization. It needs to be part of the strategy, a business imperative, and a core piece of what makes up the culture of the organization. It needs to be from a systems approach in order to enable the organization to reinvent itself. The learning and development paradigm of the 21st century must evolve from the 20th century mindset of it being an expense, and instead treat it as an investment; the future workforce consisting of more Millennials who want on-going development. Learning and development must be treated as an investment and part of a long-term strategic and human capital plan.

At the individual level, employees should not only be held accountable, but also rewarded for their continual learning and growth. An organization needs to address this proactively because it's either pay now or pay later through an "extinction event." In other words, the wrong choices now could lead to the organization disappearing.

Who better to provide learning opportunities than the leadership of organizations? In addition, leaders will need to ensure they are continually learning and modeling what they expect from their employees. Like culture and values, learning will need to enable organizations through their employees to differentiate themselves from their competitors.

Executive sponsorship and support will be crucial for change to take place and so the workforce sees the transparency and commitment modeled by the organization's leadership team. Leadership needs to create a vision for the future of the organization in order to minimize confusion. They need to ensure that they, along with their workforce, have the proper skills for success in order to minimize anxiety as people try new work practices and expectations. Lastly, leadership needs to demonstrate its support for the changes by creating an incentive for change in order to minimize resistance or gradual change. They need to ensure that the workforce and organization have the resources needed for success, in order to minimize frustration. Lastly, leadership needs to model its sponsorship and support by having an action plan in order to address these trends happening so as to minimize false starts. To use an old cliché, leadership needs to "walk the talk," and model and support what they want the organization to evolve into.

Adapting and agile practices will be needed in order to evolve. Leaders will need to constantly and quickly change scenarios; this will be something that leaders will need to become comfortable with. They will have to ensure that there are processes, a systemic and comprehensive approach, and in turn a workforce that is able and willing to adapt and remain flexible in a demanding and changing world.

Leaders will need to share information, ask for feedback, and engage in dialogue through inquiry and advocacy in order to help their employees understand the rationale for the changes. They will have to wear two hats: one focused on the here and now, and another focused on the future so they can anticipate and adapt. They will also need to arm their employees with the needed skills and resources, along with incentives (WIIFM) so that they too are adapting. This is not only important for the organization's survivability, but for the individual worker's employability. Adapting is important for all stakeholders, organizations, leaders, employees, and customers.

Agile practices are now taking hold of more organizations trying to position themselves for success by ensuring they are reinventing themselves for the 21st century world of work. What organizations will need are to have effective leaders who are able to drive change through their workforce and through effective team dynamics. "Agility is the new secret ingredient of high performing teams." (Horney, 2013).

Development is something leaders will need to ensure that their workforce has plenty of as changing needs require it. This focus is from a micro or individual perspective. Not only does this meet ongoing development needs due to constant change, such as technology and an increasingly diverse workforce, but it also meets a fundamental employee need to feel valued and relevant. With the increasing change of everything—technology, processes, customer experience and expectations, just-in-time demands, newer needed skills, access to all sort of information via the Internet—ongoing development is a key requirement.

Leaders will need to not only ensure that they are developing their staff, but also that they are developing themselves. They will need to ensure that they are assessing themselves and getting feedback so they too can continue to develop with the changing times and demands. A leader in the 21st century cannot just depend on what he or she has learned in the 20th century. Development will be continual and increasingly important to the growing Millennial workforce.

Engagement will be key for organizational success. There is enough research and anecdotal stories highlighting the business imperatives for this area along with consulting firms offering organizations support for creating an engaging workplace. From the CEO to the frontline supervisor, the environment created is important to enabling an engaged workforce.

If they aim to be successful, organizations cannot afford to focus only on their top talent and poor performers at the expense of the rest of the workforce. Both the top and bottom portions represent only 20% of the organization. Leaders must engage their entire workforce for organizational success. Leaders play a large role in creating an engaging environment. As much as some might try to attribute this to human resources, it is an organizational issue in which leadership plays a very important role.

Leaders will need to ensure they are creating an organizational culture and environment that engages everyone and considers both the macro and micro perspectives. A macro view of the environment is for the organization through its leadership to really assess what is coming into its workforce. How prepared is the workforce, and what role, if any, is the educational system playing in it? Organizations should look at some alternative approaches for working with the educational system so they are truly providing the needed workforce going forward. There needs to be some form of macrostrategic consortium that includes a partnership with corporate entities, the educational system, and the government to truly assess what the needs of the future will be and how the educational system is presently operating in preparing our workforce for that future; in essence, addressing the "elephant in the room," which is how the educational system needs to reinvent itself in order to be more efficient and effective and truly provide what the customer will need.

Another question is, how are organizations addressing the human capital challenges presented in this book? How are they preparing their workforce for the changes that will continue to occur? How are they preparing their leaders? How are they addressing employee engagement, changing demographics, new skillsets needed, diversity, and so on? They will need to scan their surroundings and ask themselves if they are really doing the right things so that they can adapt and help the workforce adapt to the increasingly changing needs.

From a micro view, leaders are almost like CEOs for their respective departments. Most employees in large organizations rarely meet their CEOs and get to see them more on company videos than in real life. But on a daily basis, the person who has an opportunity to create an engaging environment through learning, development, communications, establishing trust, and developing relationships among others is the department leader. So in a sense, the role of the leader is to serve as his or her department or organization's chief environmental officer, or to be an environmentalist.

I remember once being requested by a leader for a teaming session for assistance with his staff. He did not believe his employees were broken or inept; he just felt they needed a good teaming session. The request in itself made me wonder, since the initial request is only the beginning of what is really the issue, but I proceeded to learn more and help. It turned out that the department of six was pretty dysfunctional, demoralized, and completely upset with the manager because of his favoritism. The manager appeared to be completely clueless, or maybe he just didn't want to confront the environment he had created or permitted.

It is imperative that the department leader not stick his or her head in the sand and ignore the signals (sometimes subtle and sometimes not) of the environment that he or she is either purposely growing or allowing to grow. In the end, the department leader must work to be in tune with his or her environment. There will be things happening within the organization in other departments, but to a large extent, the department leader has more control over the department's morale and therefore environment than they are aware of. In a sense, the leader fulfills the role of an environmentalist. He or she tends to create the culture of a department.

Culture can be defined as the unwritten rules and behaviors that members of a department and organization have come to understand, accept, and live by. While all members of a department or organization accept or adapt to a given culture, the department leader plays a very important role in enabling the culture. In essence, he or she creates the backdrop that the workforce will adapt to.

Recognition and relationships are very important for leaders and employees. How leaders manage relationships, whether employees are remote or colocated with them, will affect employee engagement and result in a healthy, productive, successful environment or an unhealthy, unproductive,and unsuccessful one. There is plenty of research supporting the leadership concept of leader-employee exchange (LMX) or leader-employee relationships, which when managed effectively, lead to higher trust, increased retention, employee loyalty, higher morale, job satisfaction, productivity, and customer satisfaction (Mourino-Ruiz, 2005). So in order to achieve results and business objectives, leaders will need to ensure that they are paying attention to the relationships they have with their employees.

Most might remember having worked for someone who they considered a great boss. There was probably mutual trust and respect. Because of this, they felt they had a good relationship. At a minimum, having an effective relationship promotes leaders to Level 2 in the five levels of leadership by John Maxwell (Maxwell, 2013). At this level, people follow your lead because they want to. The challenge and opportunity is to reflect and ask yourself how you can get to the pinnacle, which is Level 5, at which people follow you because of who you are and represent.

Workers prefer a leader who is authentic, can develop effective relationships, has a genuine interest in the people who work for him or her by listening to and respecting them, and says what he or she means, and means what he or she says by keeping his or her word.

A question leaders should ask themselves is, What is my brand? How we are perceived as a leader is an interesting thought to consider. Are we seen as someone who others want to work with and for, or not? This brand will definitely have implications for the success of leaders and wannabe leaders. This leadership brand can be helped, and one can create a perception of being an effective leader by treating his or her team with respect, listening, establishing trust, transparency, and most importantly by recognizing people for doing a good job, and be in constant communications, as well as providing feedback, especially good feedback, in an ongoing manner and consistently. In a study by the Boston Consulting Group of more than 200,000 workers worldwide, the number one thing workers wanted was to be recognized (Strack, 2014).

Leaders will continue to be tremendously important in today's and tomorrow's organizations. By this, I mean "true leaders," not just in title. I have found that we sometimes diminish the importance and relevancy of effective leadership by labeling everyone, including ineffective authority figures, as leaders. How they treat their workers is a crucial ingredient in the success of their organizations. As Drucker has noted, "Management is doing things right; leadership is doing the right things." (Drucker, 2013). Both of these roles are required during this perfect storm.

The leader's success is dependent on his or her employees being successful. How he or she approaches the role of being the boss will create a department's environment and culture. If he or she believes his or her role is being the boss—the ultimate decision-maker who everyone comes to—he or she will then create a culture that is one of an outdated mode of thinking and operating.

If, on the other hand, he or she believes his or her role is one of ensuring the objectives are achieved through others' successes, that his or her employees should be treated with human dignity, and that everyone has something good and unique to contribute, he or she then can create a different culture. The leader's role is to focus on himself or herself, his or her behaviors, and how he or she comes across; on others to understand his or her perspective, and engage the leader; and on the environment or organizational culture of the organization and/or department.

The world, the United States, and the workplace as we know it is changing. This has major implications for leaders and their workforces. How they adapt to and engage in these changes will position them for success . . . or not.

For things to change, I must change.
—Mahatma Gandhi, Wildmind.org, 2006

Thoughts to reflect on:

In summary, society, organizations, and the workforce are facing dramatic changes in the future. How organizations anticipate and adapt to these changes will help determine their success. All of these changes will have macro and micro implications. It reminds me of the *Hulk* ride at Islands of Adventure in Orlando, Florida. It will be a roller coaster ride, but as we step back and reflect, it will look pretty exciting.

For those who prepare (even if not completely), the future will be pretty engaging. For those who don't, it could be pretty daunting and stressful. How one views these changing times—either as challenges or as opportunities—will definitely impact one's outlook on it all. As in *Star Trek,* now we're headed to where no one has gone before. I wish you the best.

How these changes are proactively addressed will be the difference between thriving in the future and being one of those organizations that we spoke of that once existed. What an exciting time to be engaged in the making of the present and future workplace. The key to success is to recognize and adapt for these trends and changes. In addition, you will need an engaged workforce, and to have engaged employees you will need to focus on the employee experience (Jacob, 2017).

The end, no really the beginning.

12

The Perfect Human Capital Storm Assessment

Change is all around us and a key strategic imperative for organizations. How effective is your organization? Rate the following questions by circling the appropriate number:

1. When it comes to addressing organizational changes my organization is effective.

1	2	3	4	5
Strongly Disagree	Disagree	Not sure Undecided	Agree	Strongly Agree

2. My organization is effective in implementing technological changes.

1	2	3	4	5
Strongly Disagree	Disagree	Not sure Undecided	Agree	Strongly Agree

3. When it comes to addressing the educational challenges and future workforce, my organization has been proactive and effective.

1	2	3	4	5
Strongly Disagree	Disagree	Not sure Undecided	Agree	Strongly Agree

4. My organization is proactive and effective at addressing the aging workforce.

1	2	3	4	5
Strongly Disagree	Disagree	Not sure Undecided	Agree	Strongly Agree

5. My organization prepares its leaders and workforce to be effective with the four generations in the workforce (in particular the baby boomers and Millennials).

1	2	3	4	5
Strongly Disagree	Disagree	Not sure Undecided	Agree	Strongly Agree

6. My organization has been proactive and effective at addressing the changing diversity and demographics (especially the growing Hispanic/Latino population).

1	2	3	4	5
Strongly Disagree	Disagree	Not sure Undecided	Agree	Strongly Agree

7. When it comes to addressing employee engagement, my organization is effective.

1	2	3	4	5
Strongly Disagree	Disagree	Not sure Undecided	Agree	Strongly Agree

8. When it comes to addressing leadership development issues, my organization is effective.

1	2	3	4	5
Strongly Disagree	Disagree	Not sure Undecided	Agree	Strongly Agree

Based on these ratings, what trends do you see, what insights do you gain, how well is your organization positioned for success in the 21st century and the Perfect Human Capital Storm? What can and should your leadership team do to position the organization to reinvent itself, address these changing trends, and achieve success?

References

Augustine, N., Barrett, C., Cassell, G., Chu, S., Gates, R., Grasmick, N., . . . Zare, R. (2007). *Rising above the gathering storm: Energizing and employing America for a brighter economic future.* Washington, DC: National Academies Press.

Bartiromo, M. (2013, September 16). He lifts his cup up to healthcare: Starbucks CEO takes the long view. *USA Today.*

Bersin, J. (2016a). *Future of work: The people imperative.* [Keynote from Singularity University Global Summit]. Retrieved from http://joshbersin.com/2016/11/future-of-work-the-people-imperative-keynote-from-singularity-university-global-summit/

Bersin, J. (2016b). *The future of work: It's already here—and not as scary as you think.* Retrieved from http://www.forbes.com/sites/joshbersin/2016/09/21/the-future-of-work-its-already-here-and-not-as-scary-as-you-think/#5f5e01d44bf5

Bhargava, M. (2014). *Understanding the internet of everything.* Retrieved from www.linkedin.com/pulse/article

Bodhipaksa. (2006). You must be the change you wish to see in the world. Retrieved from http://www.wildmind.org/blogs/quote-of-the-month/quote-gandhi

Bordas, J. (2013). *The power of Latino leadership: Culture, inclusion, and contribution.* San Francisco, CA: Berrett-Koehler.

Branham, L. (2005). *The 7 hidden reasons employees leave.* New York, NY: Amacon.

Buchanan, L. (2013, June). Between Venus and Mars: 7 traits of true leaders. *Inc. Magazine, 35*(5).

Burrell, L. (2016). We just can't handle diversity. *Harvard Business Review, 94*(July/August), 70–74.

The Perfect Human Capital Storm, pages 63–68
Copyright © 2017 by Information Age Publishing

Cartagena, C. (2013). *The Latino boom II: Catching the biggest demographic wave since the baby boom.* New York, NY: Custom Worthy.

Casio, W. (2015). *Managing human resources: Productivity, quality of work, life, and profits* (10th ed.). New York, NY: McGraw-Hill.

Cohn, D. (2015). Future immigration will change the face of America by 2065. *Pew Research.* Retrieved from http://www.pewresearch.org/fact-tank/2015/10/05/future-immigration-will-change-the-face-of-america-by-2065/

Colvin, G. (2015). *Humans are underrated: What high achievers know that brilliant machines never will.* New York, NY: Random House.

Covey, S. (2014). BrainyQuotes. Retrieved from https://www.brainyquote.com/quotes/quotes/s/stephencov636520.html

Cummings, T,. & Worley, C. (2008). *Organization development & change.* Stamford, CT: Cengage Learning.

Diamandis, P., & Kotler, S. (2012). *Abundance: The future is better then you think.* New York, NY: Free Press.

Drucker, P. (2013). Management is doing things right; leadership is doing the right things. BrainyQuotes. Retrieved from www.izquotes.com.

DuBrin, A. J. (2014). *Leadership: Research findings, practice, and skills* (8th ed.). Boston, MA: Cengage Learning.

Erickson, T. (2014, January 14). Hispanic talent is the future for big companies. *Harvard Business Review.* Retrieved from https://hbr.org/2014/01/hispanic-talent-is-the-future-for-big-companies

Frank, M., Roehrig, P., & Pring, B. (2014). *Code halos: How the digital lives of people, things, and organizations are changing the rules of business.* Hoboken, NJ: Wiley,.

Frey, C., & Osborne, M. (2013). *The future of employment: How susceptible are jobs to computerization?* Oxford Martin School. Retrieved from http://www.oxfordmartin.ox.ac.uk/downloads/academic/The_Future_of_Employment.pdf

Friedman, T. (2011, September 4). *Meet the Press.*

Frohlich, T. (2014). The most educated countries in the world. *USAToday.* Retrieved from http://www.usatoday.com/story/money/business/2014/09/13/24-7-wall-st-most-educated-countries/15460733/

Garcia, R. (2015). *When technology blurs human values.* Retrieved from https://www.linkedin.com/pulse/when-technology-blurs-human-values-ray-garcia

Garvin, D. (2013, December). How Google sold its engineers on management. *Harvard Business Review.* Retrieved from https://hbr.org/2013/12/how-google-sold-its-engineers-on-management

Gentry, W., Eckert, R., Stawiski, S. & Zhao, S. (2016). The challenges leaders face around the world: More similar than different [White paper]. *Center for Creative Leadership.* Retrieved from http://www.ccl.org/wp-content/uploads/2015/04/ChallengesLeadersFace.pdf

Gordon, E. (2012). The talent hunters: China, India, and U.S. vie for skilled workers. *The Futurist, 46*(4).

Gordon, E. (2013). *Future jobs: Solving the employment and skills crisis.* Westport, CT: Praeger.

Grossman, L. (2011). 2045: The year man becomes immortal. *Time.* Retrieved from http://content.time.com/time/magazine/article/0,9171,2048299,00.html

Harter, J., Schmidt, F., Killham, E., & Agrawal, S. (2009). *Q12 meta-analysis: The relationship between engagement at work and organizational outcomes.* Gallup.

Hay Group. (2012). *Why does employee engagement matter to CEOs?*

Heinen, J., & Wiete, A. (2012, December). *Scaling executive coaching across the enterprise.* Cincinnati, OH: Human Capital Institute. Retrieved from http://www.hci.org/lib/scaling-executive-coaching-across-enterprise

Hesselbein, F., & Goldsmith, M. (Eds.). (2009). *The organization of the future 2: Visions, strategies, and insights on managing in a new era.* Hoboken, NJ: Wiley.

Horney, N. (2013). *Agility: The new secret ingredient for high performing teams.* Strategic Agility Institute (SAI). Retrieved from: http://agilityconsulting.com

Indeed. (2016). *16 trends shaping the global economy (and how you hire)* [Blog]. Retrieved from http://blog.indeed.com/2016/06/22/global-economy-employment-trends/

Ito, J. (2014). Want to innovate? Become a "nowist." *TED Talk.* Retrieved from https://www.ted.com/talks/joi_ito_want_to_innovate_become_a_now_ist

Jackson, R., Howe, N., & Nakashima, K. (2011). *Global aging and the future of emerging markets.* Washington, DC: Center for Strategic & International Studies (CSIS).

James, J. (2015). Data never sleeps 3.0. *DOMO.* Retrieved from https://www.domo.com/blog/data-never-sleeps-3-0/

Kotter, J. (2007, January). Leading change: Why transformations fail. *Harvard Business Review.* Retrieved from https://hbr.org/2007/01/leading-change-why-transformation-efforts-fail

Krugstad, J., Passel, J., & Cohn, D. (2016). 5 facts about illegal immigration in the U.S. *Pew Research.* Retrieved from http://www.pewresearch.org/fact-tank/2016/11/03/5-facts-about-illegal-immigration-in-the-u-s/

Locsin, A. (2014). *Comparison of level of education to salary.* Retrieved from www.work.chron.com

Mackey, J., & Sisodia, R. (2014). *Conscious capitalism: Liberating the heroic spirit of business.* Boston, MA: Harvard Business School Publishing.

Maitland, A., & Thomson, P. (2011). *Future work: How businesses can adapt and thrive in the new world of work.* New York, NY: Palgrave Macmillan.

Maurer, R. (2010). *Beyond the wall of resistance.* Austin, TX: Bard Press.

Maxwell, J. (2013). *The 5 levels of leadership.* New York, NY: Center Street.

Meachum, J. (2013, October 7). Class of 2025: How they'll learn and what they'll pay. *Time.*

Meister, J., & Willyerd, K., (2010). *The 2020 workplace: How innovative companies attract, develop, and keep tomorrow's employees today.* New York, NY: HarperBusiness.

Merchant, N. (2011, March 22). Culture trumps strategy every time [Blog post]. *Business Insider.* Retrieved from http://www.businessinsider.com/culture-trumps-strategy-every-time-2011-3

Morgan, J. (2014). *The future of work: Attract new talent, build better leaders, and create a competitive organization.* Hoboken, NJ: Wiley.

Morgan, J. (2016). The 5 trends shaping the future of work. *YouTube.* Retrieved from https://www.youtube.com/watch?v=LrhmHbDLM8o

Morgan, J. (2017). *Employee experience advantage: How to win the war for talent by giving employees the workspace they want, the tools they need, and a culture they can celebrate.* Hoboken, NJ: Wiley.

Morgan, L. (2004). *Driving performance and retention through employee engagement: Study.* Corporate Leadership Council. Retrieved from: http://www.three-squared.com/client_review/Novelis/LAC/Revised/assets/Driving%20 Performance%20and%20Retention%20Through%20Employee%20 Engagement.pdf

Mouriño-Ruiz, E. (2005). *The impact of effective leader-member exchange (LMX) on virtual and collocated employee relationships* (Doctoral dissertation). Barry University.

Murray, A. (2015, October 22). Six fundamental truths about the 21st century corporation. *Fortune.* Retrieved from http://fortune.com/2015/10/22/six-truths-21st-century-corporation/

Murray, A. (2016, June 3). The biggest challenge facing Fortune 500 companies. *Fortune.* Retrieved from http://fortune.com/2016/06/03/challenges -facing-fortune-500/?iid=sr-link1

Nassar, H., Johnson, K., & Lichter, D. (2009, June 17). Analysis of 2008 census estimates. *USA Today.*

O'Donnell, J. (2013, June 9). Offices try to adjust to Gen y's 'But why?' attitudes. *USA Today.*

OneIndia. (2016). *Fake degree case: Court asks EC to authenticate certificates of Smriti Irani.* Retrieved from http://www.oneindia.com/india/fake-degree-day-reckoning-smriti-irani-former-hrd-minister-controversy-2228356.html

Pane, J. Steiner, E., Baird, M., & Hamilton, L. (2015). Continued progress: Promising evidence on personalized learning. *Rand Corporation.* Retrieved from http://www.rand.org/pubs/research_reports/RR1365.html

Pew Research. (2015). *Where each state's largest immigrant population was born.* Retrieved from http://www.pewresearch.org/fact-tank/2015/10/07/a-shift-from-germany-to-mexico-for-americas-immigrants/ft_15-10-07 _germmexicoblogupdate/

Pfau, B. (2016, April 7). What do millennials really want at work? The same thing the rest of us do. *Harvard Business Review.* Retrieved from https://hbr.org/2016/04/what-do-millennials-really-want-at-work

Pfeffer, J. (2010, February 15). Layoffs are bad for business: The downside of downsizing. *Newsweek.*

Pritchett, R., & Pound, R. (2008). *The employee handbook for organizational change.* Dallas, TX: Pritchett.

Robbins, T. (2006, June 14). Nearly half of illegal immigrants overstay visas. *NPR: All Things Considered.* Retrieved from http://www.npr.org/templates/story/story.php?storyId=5485917

Robinson, K. (2010). Changing education paradigms. *TED Talks.* Retrieved from http://www.ted.com/talks/ken_robinson_changing_education_paradigms

Rock, D. (2013, October). Why organizations fail. *Fortune.*

Rodriguez, R. (2007). *Latino talent-effective strategies to recruit, retain, and develop Hispanic professionals.* New York, NY: Wiley.

Roehrig, P., & Pring, B. (2012). *Building a modern social enterprise to win in the 21st century.* Teaneck, NJ: Cognizant.

Royal, M., & Stark, M. (2016). How the world's most admired companies are preparing for the future. *Fortune.* Retrieved from http://fortune.com/2016/02/19/worlds-most-admired-companies-preparing-future/

Senge, P. (2010). *The fifth discipline: The art and practice of the learning organization.* New York, NY: Crown

Shervani, T. (2014). *Four markets: How global forces are reshaping economies, companies, and networks.* Retrieved from http://tia2014.org/sites/default/files/pages/Globalization%20TIA_widescreen_June%204%202014.pdf.

Slocum, D. (2013). Six creative leadership lessons from the military in an era of VUCA and COIN. *Forbes.* Retrieved from http://www.forbes.com/sites/berlinschoolofcreativeleadership/2013/10/08/six-creative-leadership-lessons-from-the-military-in-an-era-of-vuca-and-coin/#14b6360a3b2a

Smikle, J. (2016). *Transformational leadership: The key to employee engagement and commitment.* Retrieved from http://www.smiklespeaks.com/files/articles/HRKY_Fall14.pdf

Strack, R. (2014). The workforce crisis of 2030—and how to start solving it now. *TED Talks.* Retrieved from http://www.ted.com/talks/rainer_strack_the_surprising_workforce_crisis_of_2030_and_how_to_start_solving_it_now

Tapia, A. (2012, July/August). Habla español? *Diversity Executive Magazine.*

Tapscott, D. (2008). *Grown up digital: How the net generation is changing your world.* New York, NY: McGraw-Hill.

The Economist. (2015, May 9). The dawn of artificial intelligence. Retrieved from http://www.economist.com/news/leaders/21650543-powerful-computers-will-reshape-humanitys-future-how-ensure-promise-outweighs

Univision Documentary, Al Punto. (2013, October 6). *La ultima frontera: La crisis de la educacion hispana.* Retrieved from http://www.univision.com/noticias/adelanto-la-ultima-frontera-video

Wendel, S. (2014, June). An employer's guide to employee engagement. *Hello Wallet.* Retrieved from http://info.hellowallet.com/rs/hellowallet/images/HelloWallet%20-%20An%20Employers%20Guide%20To%20Employee%20Engagement.pdf?mkt_tok=3RkMMJWWfF9wsRonva7KZKXo

njHpfsX56eguW6S2lMI%2F0ER3fOvrPUfGjI4AScBrI%2BSLDwEYGJlv6S
gFSLDDMbJn0LgNUhc%3D

Xavier, S. (2009, April 26). The dark side of the retirement bubble. *Chief Learning Officer*. Retrieved from http://www.clomedia.com/2009/04/26/the-dark-side-of-the-retirement-bubble/

Yip, J., Ernst, C., & Campbell, M. (2011). Boundary spanning leadership. *Center for Creative Leadership* [White paper]. Retrieved from http://insights.ccl.org/wp-content/uploads/2015/04/BoundarySpanningLeadership.pdf.

Made in the USA
Middletown, DE
15 July 2017